EARLY TO MID-INTERMEDIATE

COMPOSER'S CHOICE

ERIC BAUMGARTNER

ABOUT THE SERIES

The Composer's Choice series ___ ___ works by an exclusive group of comp___ ___ ___ins classic piano pieces that were car___ ___ ___omposer, as well as brand-new pieces writte___ ___ ___ly for the series. Helpful performance notes are also included.

ISBN 978-1-4803-0863-3

WILLIS MUSIC

EXCLUSIVELY DISTRIBUTED BY

HAL•LEONARD® CORPORATION

7777 W. BLUEMOUND RD. P.O. BOX 13819 MILWAUKEE, WI 53213

Visit Hal Leonard Online at
www.halleonard.com

FROM THE COMPOSER

This collection contains six of my favorite pieces along with two new compositions. I've strived to select pieces that are not only fun to play but that also represent a variety of styles. It is my hope that you'll enjoy performing these compositions as much as I did writing them.

Eric Baumgartner

CONTENTS

6 THE CUCKOO

8 SCHERZANDO

10 NEW ORLEANS NOCTURNE

12 GOBLIN DANCE

16 JOURNEY'S END

18 ARETTA'S RHUMBA

21 JACKRABBIT RAMBLE

26 BEALE STREET BOOGIE

BY ERIC BAUMGARTNER

THE CUCKOO

Bird calls have fascinated musicians for ages. There are many examples of birdsong in composition, from the simple (Beethoven's 6th Symphony) to the complex (Messiaen's *Oiseaux Exotiques*). "The Cuckoo" employs some simple calls in the A section and coda. Although marked *Moderato*, I encourage the performer to experiment with faster tempi to evoke a more animated bird!

SCHERZANDO

The challenge in this piece is to keep it light and playful at a fast tempo. It requires a nimble touch with dynamics that never rise above mezzo forte. Work for consistent and smooth 16th notes. Control of these 16th-note phrases is key to performing at a lightning-fast tempo.

NEW ORLEANS NOCTURNE

I've always loved compositions that make temporary tonal shifts to different keys only to cleverly return to the tonic (Jerome Kern and Elton John were particularly good at this practice). In "New Orleans Nocturne" I made a conscious decision to explore shifting tonalities in the A section while trying to retain a cohesive structure and melody. The accidentals sprinkled throughout are the easiest way to identify these tonal shifts.

GOBLIN DANCE

"Goblin Dance" is inspired by some of the more playful pieces by Edvard Grieg (particularly "Puck" and "Elfin Dance") as well as by the progressive rock band Gentle Giant. Pay close attention to the varied articulation and dynamics to help bring out the mischief!

JOURNEY'S END

This lyrical piece benefits from a sensitive touch. Follow the course of the melody between both hands and be sure to keep it legato for a smooth, cantabile style. Although dynamics and tempo variations are marked throughout, your teacher may help you find additional opportunities to 'push and pull' the tempo as well as add crescendo and diminuendo to various phrases.

ARETTA'S RHUMBA

This piece is a gift to my wife, Aretta. It is a lively dance inspired by her vivacious personality. Latin jazz contains much of the syncopations and rich harmonies of American jazz but usually uses straight 8th notes rather than swing. Should these rhythms prove to be a challenge (they are tricky!), I suggest working very slowly in 4/4 before increasing the tempo to cut-time. Special rhythmic attention may be needed in the section beginning with measure 25. Many of these phrases contain notes only on the offbeats. Be sure to count out the quarter-note pulse to better feel the placement of the notes.

JACKRABBIT RAMBLE

"Jackrabbit Ramble" employs a left-hand stride piano technique common in ragtime. The left hand supplies a steady quarter-note anchor for the right hand's syncopated melody. Keep the left hand light and detached (not a full staccato) and bring out the right-hand melody. The tempo indication "with reckless abandon" encourages a very bright speed. Once you have control of all the elements, go for it!

BEALE STREET BOOGIE

Ooh, this is a fun one! It is in the boogie-woogie or barrelhouse style of piano characterized by a steady left-hand ostinato figure (the figure is a common one found in many boogies). The form is a 12-bar blues. You'll, therefore, notice the left-hand pattern jump from the I (C) to the IV (F) to the V (G). Boogie-woogie relies on a rock solid left-hand accompaniment. The pattern should be practiced alone until it is on "automatic pilot." It will then be easier to add the right-hand chords and melodies.

The Cuckoo

Eric Baumgartner

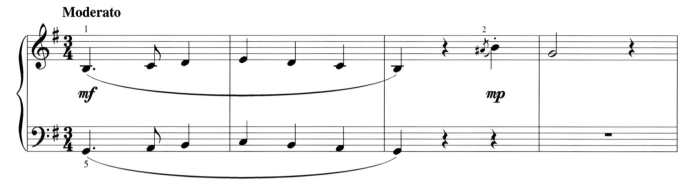

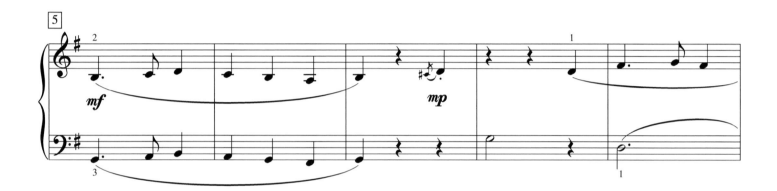

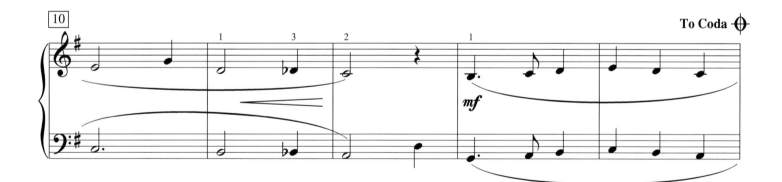

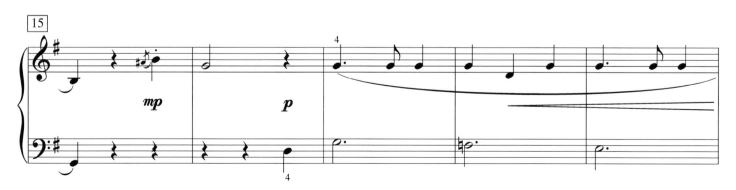

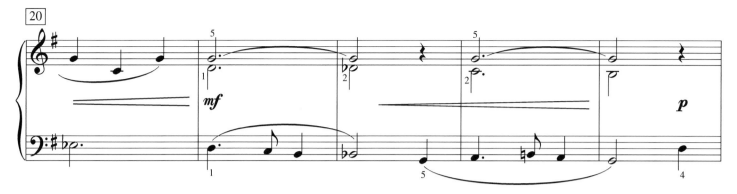

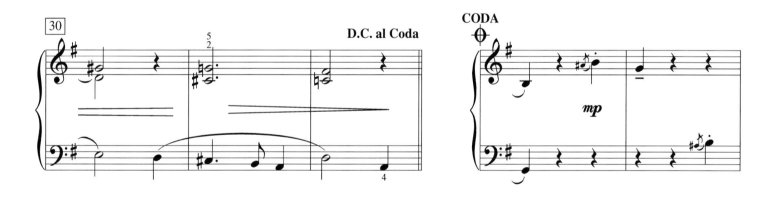

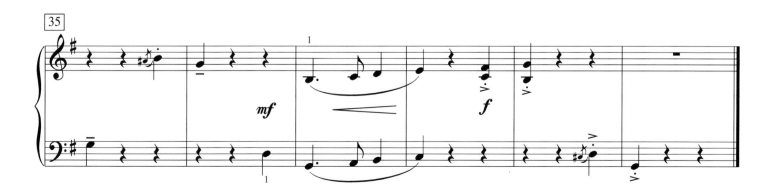

Scherzando

Eric Baumgartner

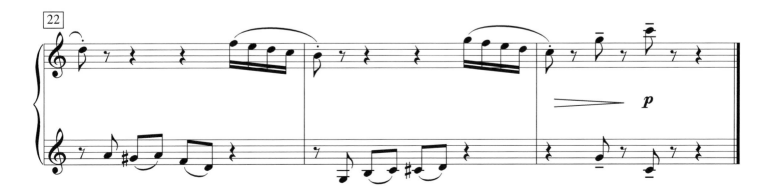

New Orleans Nocturne

Eric Baumgartner

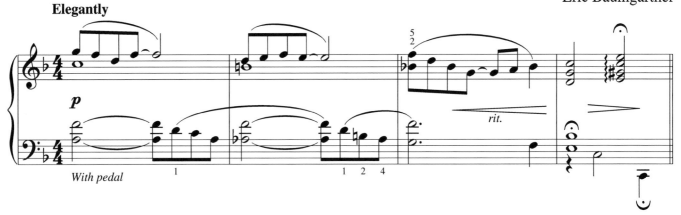

Goblin Dance

Eric Baumgartner

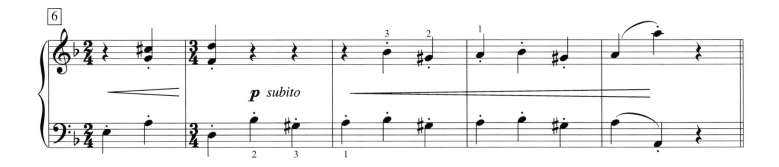

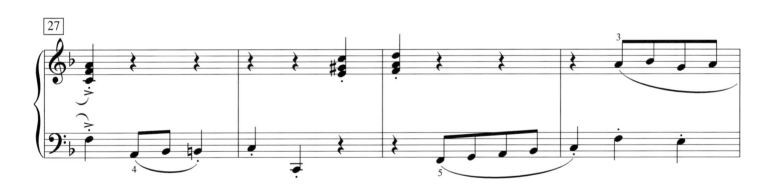

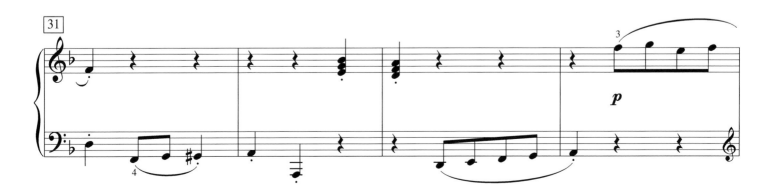

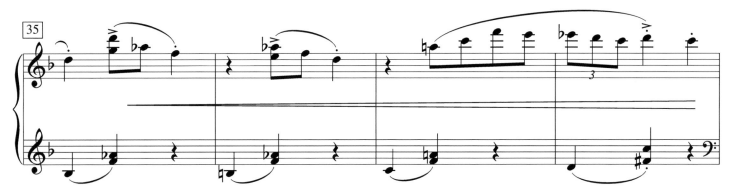

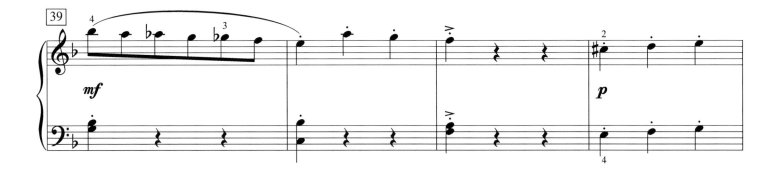

Journey's End

Eric Baumgartner

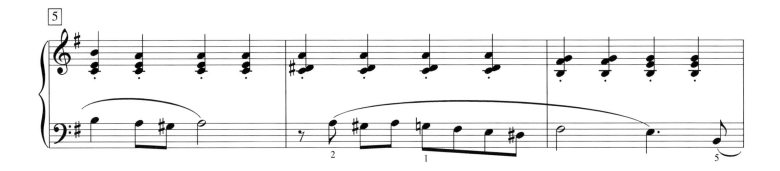

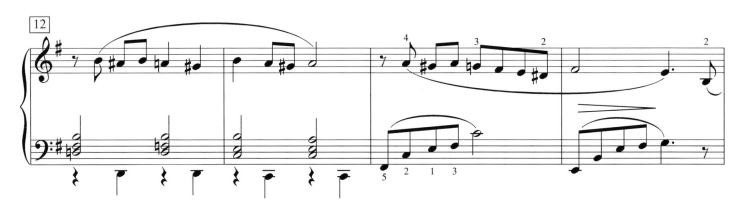

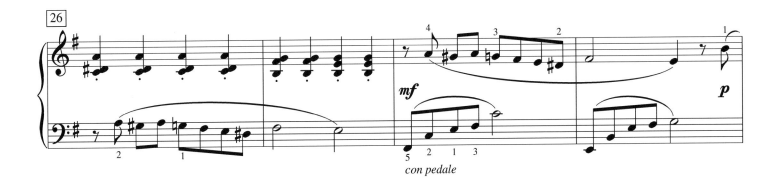

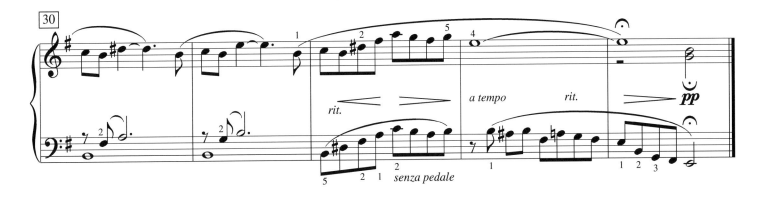

Aretta's Rhumba

for my wonderful 'Esposa'

Eric Baumgartner

Moderately fast Latin jazz

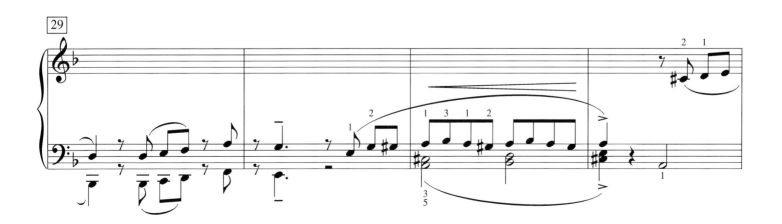

Jackrabbit Ramble

for my cousin Beverly Coates

Eric Baumgartner

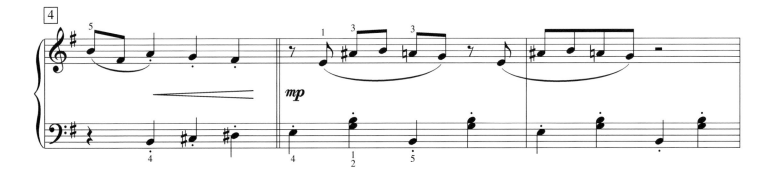

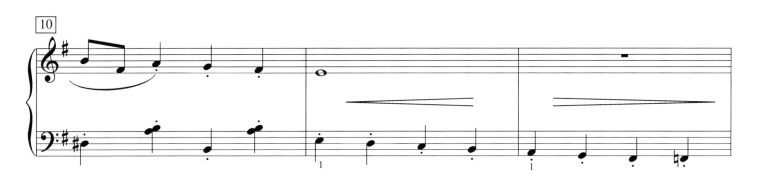

Beale Street Boogie

Eric Baumgartner

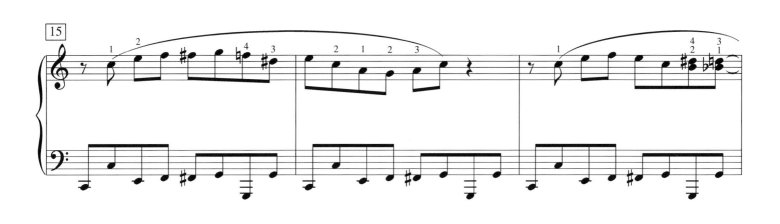

Spectacular Piano Solos

from

www.willispianomusic.com

Early Elementary

00416850	Barnyard Strut/*Glenda Austin*	$2.99
00416702	Big Green Frog/*Carolyn C. Setliff*	$2.99
00416904	The Blizzard/*Glenda Austin*	$2.99
00416882	Bow-Wow Blues/*Glenda Austin*	$2.99
00406670	Cookies/*Carolyn Miller*	$2.99
00404218	Fog at Sea/*William Gillock*	$2.99
00416907	Guardian Angels/*Naoko Ikeda*	$3.99
00416918	Halloween Surprise/*Ronald Bennett*	$2.99
00412099	Moccasin Dance/*John Thompson*	$2.99
00416783	My Missing Teeth/*Carolyn C. Setliff*	$2.95
00416933	The Perceptive Detective/*Carolyn Miller*	$2.99
00416816	Rain, Rain/*Carolyn Miller*	$2.99

Mid-Elementary

00416780	The Acrobat/*Carolyn Miller*	$2.99
00416041	Autumn Is Here/*William Gillock*	$3.99
00416803	The Dancing Bears/*Carolyn Miller*	$2.99
00416878	Mini Toccata/*Eric Baumgartner*	$2.99
00416958	Miss Kitty Kat/*Glenda Austin*	$2.99
00404738	Moonlight/*William Gillock*	$3.99
00416872	The Rainbow/*Carolyn Miller*	$2.99
00416728	Seahorse Serenade/*Carolyn C. Setliff*	$2.95
00416674	Seaside Dancer/*Ronald Bennett*	$2.50

Later Elementary

00416852	Black Cat Chat/*Eric Baumgartner*	$2.99
00416786	Egyptian Journey/*Randall Hartsell*	$2.95
00416906	Evening Melody/*Naoko Ikeda*	$3.99
00416886	Flying Fingers/*Carolyn C. Setliff*	$3.99
00416836	The Gentle Brook/*Carolyn Miller*	$2.99
00416908	The Goblins Gather/*Frank Levin*	$2.99
00405918	Monkey on a Stick/*Lynn Freeman Olson*	$2.95
00416866	October Leaves/*Carolyn C. Setliff*	$2.99
00406552	Parisian Waltz/*Robert Donahue*	$2.95
00416781	The Race Car/*Carolyn Miller*	$2.99
00406564	Showdown/*Ronald Bennett*	$2.99
00416919	Sparkling Waterfall/*Carolyn C. Setliff*	$2.99
00416820	Star Wonders/*Randall Hartsell*	$2.99
00416779	Sunrise at San Miguel/*Ronald Bennett*	$3.99
00416881	Twilight Tarantella/*Glenda Austin*	$2.99

Early Intermediate

00416943	Autumn Nocturne/*Susan Alcon*	$2.99
00405455	Bass Train Boogie/*Stephen Adoff*	$2.99
00416817	Broken Arm Blues/*Carolyn Miller*	$2.99
00416841	The Bubbling Brook/*Carolyn Miller*	$2.99
00416849	Bye-Bye Blues/*Glenda Austin*	$2.99
00416945	Cafe Francais/*Jonathan Maiocco*	$2.99
00416834	Canopy of Stars/*Randall Hartsell*	$2.99
00416956	Dancing in a Dream/*William Gillock*	$3.99
00415585	Flamenco/*William Gillock*	$2.99
00416856	Garden of Dreams/*Naoko Ikeda*	$2.99
00416818	Majestic Splendor/*Carolyn C. Setliff*	$2.99
00416948	Manhattan Swing/*Naoko Ikeda*	$2.99
00416733	The Matador/*Carolyn Miller*	$3.99

00416940	Medieval Rondo/*Carolyn C. Setliff*	$2.99
00416942	A Melancholy Night/*Naoko Ikeda*	$3.99
00416877	Mystic Quest/*Randall Hartsell*	$2.99
00416873	Le Papillon (The Butterfly)/*Glenda Austin*	$2.99
00416829	Scherzo Nuovo/*Eric Baumgartner*	$2.99
00416947	Snowflakes in Spring/*Naoko Ikeda*	$2.99
00416937	Stampede/*Carolyn Miller*	$2.99
00416917	Supernova/*Ronald Bennett*	$2.99
00416842	Tarantella in G Minor/*Glenda Austin*	$3.99
00416782	Toccata Caprice/*Carolyn C. Setliff*	$2.95
00416938	Toccatina Tag/*Ronald Bennett*	$2.99
00416869	Twilight Tapestry/*Randall Hartsell*	$2.99
00416924	A Waltz to Remember/*Glenda Austin*	$3.99

Mid-Intermediate

00416911	Blues Streak/*Eric Baumgartner*	$2.99
00416855	Dance of the Unicorn/*Naoko Ikeda*	$2.99
00416893	Fantasia in A Minor/*Randall Hartsell*	$2.99
00416821	Foggy Blues/*Naoko Ikeda*	$3.99
00414908	Fountain in the Rain/*William Gillock*	$3.99
00416765	Grand Sonatina in G/*Glenda Austin*	$2.95
00416875	Himalayan Grandeur/*Randall Hartsell*	$2.99
00406630	Jazz Suite No. 2/*Glenda Austin*	$4.99
00416910	Little Rock (& Roll)/*Eric Baumgartner*	$3.99
00416939	Midnight Fantasy/*Carolyn C. Setliff*	$2.99
00416857	Moonlight Rose/*Naoko Ikeda*	$2.99
00414627	Portrait of Paris/*William Gillock*	$2.99
00405171	Sea Nocturne/*Glenda Austin*	$2.99
00416844	Sea Tempest/*Randall Hartsell*	$2.99
00415517	Sonatine/*William Gillock*	$4.99
00416701	Spanish Romance/*arr. Frank Levin*	$2.95
00416946	Stormy Seas/*Carolyn Miller*	$3.99
00416100	Three Jazz Preludes/*William Gillock*	$4.99

Later Intermediate

00416764	Romantic Rhapsody/*Glenda Austin*	$4.99
00405646	Soft Lights/*Carolyn Jones Campbell*	$2.99
00409464	Tarantella/*A. Pieczonka*	$3.99

Early Advanced

00415263	Impromptu/*Mildred T. Souers*	$2.99
00415166	Sleighbells in the Snow/*William Gillock*	$4.99
00405264	Valse Brillante/*Glenda Austin*	$4.99

7777 W. BLUEMOUND RD. P.O. BOX 13819 MILWAUKEE, WI 53213

CLOSER LOOK View sample pages and hear audio excerpts online at **www.halleonard.com**

 www.facebook.com/willispianomusic

Prices & availability subject to change without notice.